P9-CDE-663

THE SUPER SCIENCE BOOK OF

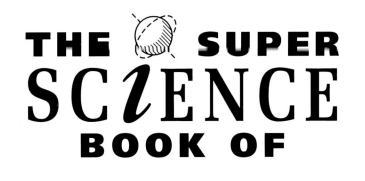

MATERIALS

Graham Peacock and Cally Chambers

Materials

*I built a castle out of rain
With rubber bands for windowpanes,
And in the gardens all around
I planted sunbeams in the ground.*

*Summer came and roses grew
Metal petals, white-hot dew,
Dragonflies stop-starting past
Over waterfalls of glass.*

*In the winter, I made do
With icicles instead of glue
To stick the stars on to a sky
Of custard creams and apple pie.*

*And when at last all was complete
I snipped the corners, made it neat,
Wrapped my world in sheets of mist,
Sealed and sent it with a kiss.*

Illustrations by Frances Lloyd

Thomson Learning • New York

Titles in the Super Science series

Light
Materials
Our Bodies
Space
Time
Weather

First published in the United States in 1993 by
Thomson Learning
115 Fifth Avenue
New York, NY 10003

First published in 1993 by
Wayland (Publishers) Ltd.

Library of Congress Cataloging-in-Publication Data
Peacock, Graham.
  The super science book of materials / Graham Peacock and
Cally Chambers; illustrations by Frances Lloyd.
        p.   cm. – (Super science)
  Includes bibliographical references and index.
  ISBN 1-56847-096-7 : $14.95
  1. Materials – Juvenile literature. [1. Materials –
Experiments. 2. Experiments.] I. Peacock, Graham. II Lloyd,
Frances, ill. III. Title. IV. Series.
TA402.3.C48   1993
620.1'1 – dc20   93-30779

Printed in Italy

Series Editors: Cally Chambers and James Kerr
Designer: Loraine Hayes Design

Picture acknowledgments

Illustrations by Frances Lloyd.
Cover illustration by Martin Gordon.

Photographs by permission of: Cephas Picture Library 23
(Ted Stefan), 24 (Mick Rock); Bruce Coleman Ltd. 19 top
(L.C. Marigo), 21 (Andy Purcell); E.T. Archive 19 bottom;
Explorer 10 (D. Auvray), 22 (Roy); Eye Ubiquitous 15 (TRIP);
PHOTRI 17; Science Photo Library 16 top (Richard
Megna/Fundamental Photos), bottom (J. G. Paren); Tony
Stone Worldwide 6 (Rohan), 12 (David Sutherland), 13
(Mike Botha), 14 (Gary Irving), 25 (Paul Chesley), 27 top
(Greg Pease) bottom (Keith Wood), 29 (Jess Stock); Wayland
Picture Library 4 both, 5, 8, 26.

CONTENTS

SOLIDS, LIQUIDS, AND GASES

Look around your kitchen at home and think of all the solids, liquids, and gases you use.

◀ Solid materials keep their shape. We choose different solid materials to do particular jobs. Some solids are useful because they are very hard, like the metal used to make knives and forks or the china used to make plates. Some solids are soft, like butter and margarine.

Liquids are runny and do not keep their shape. They will spread over a flat surface or take on the shape of the container into which they are poured.

Some liquids, like water, are very runny and spread out very quickly. Others, like this dishwashing liquid, are thicker and spread slowly. ▶

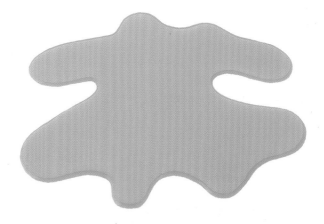

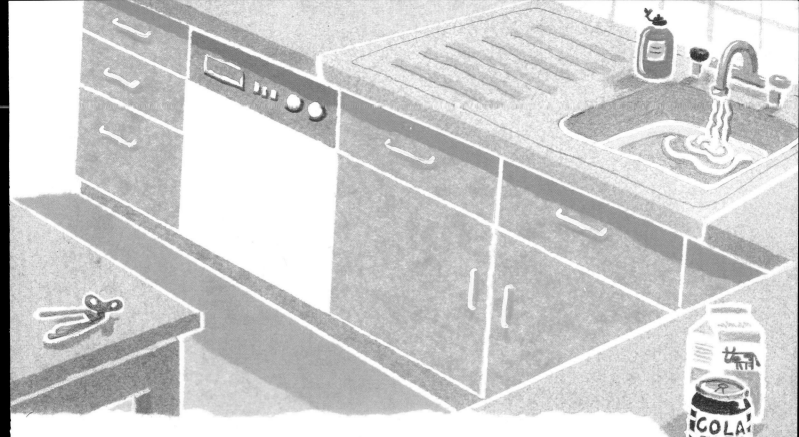

You are completely surrounded by a mixture of gases, called air, that you breathe. A gas will spread out as much as possible to fill even the largest container. Some people use natural gas for cooking.

This fizzy drink contains a solid, a ▶ liquid, and a gas. The solid is ice. The liquid is water. The gas is lots of tiny bubbles of carbon dioxide, which give the drink its fizz.

WOW!
Water is the only material that is found naturally on earth as a solid, liquid, and gas.

ATOMS AND MOLECULES

All substances are made from molecules. A molecule is the smallest particle of a substance that can also exist by itself. Even though it is too small for the eye to see, a molecule is made up of even smaller parts called atoms. Two thousand years ago the Greeks were the first people to propose that atoms existed. However, to this day no one has ever seen an atom because no microscope has been invented that can see such tiny things.

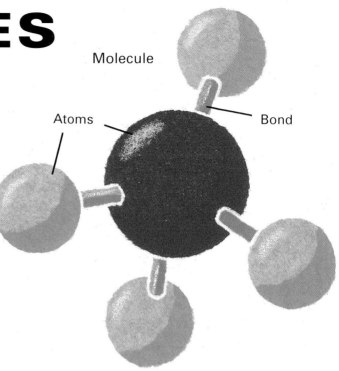

Molecule

Atoms

Bond

▲ Atoms usually join together to form molecules. The atoms are attracted to one another, and the pull between them is very strong. The pulling forces, called bonds, hold the atoms together.

◄ This is the Atomium Building in Brussels, Belgium. It was built to give people an idea of how atoms join together to make one molecule. We can think of each ball shape as one atom. The rods joining them together show where the bonds are, although bonds in real life are invisible forces.

LEMENTs AND
COMPOUNDS

A molecule of the element oxygen.

Some molecules are made up of only one type of atom. Some are made up of a combination of different atoms.

A material made from only one kind of ▶ atom is called an element. Hydrogen and oxygen, which are gases, are two examples of elements.

A molecule of the element hydrogen.

The periodic table
More than 110 different elements exist, and each one has its own chemical symbol. To help remember what each element is like, scientists arrange the elements in a huge table, called the periodic table. Groups of elements that share similar properties are sometimes color-coded. Every substance in the world is made up of one or more of these elements joined together in different ways.

1 H																	2 He
3 Li	4 Be											5 B	6 C	7 N	8 O	9 F	10 Ne
11 Na	12 Mg											13 Al	14 Si	15 P	16 S	17 Cl	18 Ar
19 K	20 Ca	21 Sc	22 Ti	23 V	24 Cr	25 Mn	26 Fe	27 Co	28 Ni	29 Cu	30 Zn	31 Ga	32 Ge	33 As	34 Se	35 Br	36 Kr
37 Rb	38 Sr	39 Y	40 Zr	41 Nb	42 Mo	43 Tc	44 Ru	45 Rh	46 Pd	47 Ag	48 Cd	49 In	50 Sn	51 Sb	52 Te	53 I	54 Xe
55 Cs	56 Ba	57 La	72 Hf	73 Ta	74 W	75 Re	76 Os	77 Ir	78 Pt	79 Au	80 Hg	81 Tl	82 Pb	83 Bi	84 Po	85 At	86 Rn
87 Fr	88 Ra	89 Ac															

58 Ce	59 Pr	60 Nd	61 Pm	62 Sm	63 Eu	64 Gd	65 Tb	66 Dy	67 Ho	68 Er	69 Tm	70 Yb	71 Lu
90 Th	91 Pa	92 U	93 Np	94 Pu	95 Am	96 Cm	97 Bk	98 Cf	99 Es	100 Fm	101 Md	102 No	103 Lr

A molecule of the compound water.

A molecule of the compound carbon dioxide.

If a substance is made up of a ▶ mixture of elements, it is called a compound. Water is made up of hydrogen and oxygen atoms. Carbon dioxide, which is a gas, is made up of carbon and oxygen atoms. Water and carbon dioxide are examples of simple compounds.

EXPANDING

Just as there are forces, or bonds, that pull and hold atoms to make molecules, there are similar forces that act between the molecules themselves.

Molecules are like vibrating balls. They have energy that makes them jiggle to and fro. Sometimes they have so much energy that the pulling forces between the molecules are not strong enough to hold them close together. The molecules wobble and bounce apart. When the molecules have less energy, the forces between them can pull them together and hold them in place more easily.

Heat is a kind of energy. If a substance is heated, the molecules that make up the substance vibrate and wobble a lot. They move apart and spread out. As they do this the substance expands, or becomes larger. The molecules themselves don't become larger – just the spaces between them.

▲ In very hot weather the Eiffel Tower in Paris, France, is 4 inches taller than when it is cold. This is because the heat makes the solid metal expand.

◀ Gases can expand too. In the eighteenth century the Montgolfier brothers discovered that a bag or balloon could be made to rise. A balloon was filled with air heated by a fire. The heat made the air expand and take up more space. This made the air in the balloon lighter than the air outside, so the balloon floated up into the sky.

AND
CONTRACTING

When a material cools down, its molecules have less energy. They slow down and vibrate less. The forces between the molecules can pull them tightly together. The material contracts, or becomes smaller.

Expansion and contraction can be useful. Most thermometers can measure temperature because the liquid inside them expands and contracts as it gets hotter or colder. The liquid is held in a bulb at the bottom of the thermometer and moves up and down a narrow tube as the temperature changes. Markings on the tube show what the temperature is.

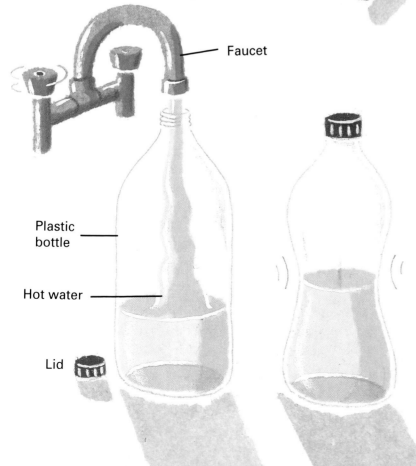

Faucet

Plastic bottle

Hot water

Lid

Watching contraction

1 Fill a plastic bottle with fairly hot tap water to about one-third full. Screw the lid on tightly. Be careful when using hot water. Ask an adult to help you.

2 Put the bottle in a cool place (but not in the refrigerator). Look at it after about 30 minutes. Can you explain why the bottle has caved in?

MELTING AND FREEZING

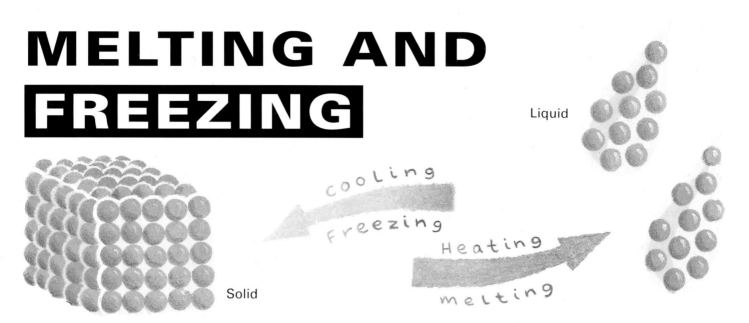

Liquid

cooling

Freezing

Heating

melting

Solid

Heat and cooling can change a material into a solid, liquid, or gas.

On a very cold winter's day you may see ice and snow around you. This is water as a solid. The water molecules have been frozen into fixed positions. If the weather warms up, the ice melts and becomes liquid water. The warmth weakens the pull between the water molecules and lets them move freely as a liquid.

Every year in Japan there is a snow festival. Huge sculptures are carved out of solid ice. These large men are characters found in Japanese theater. As long as the air temperature stays below freezing point (32°F), the sculptures will stay frozen. ▶

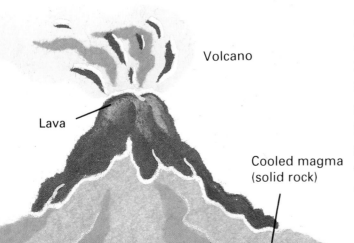

Volcano

Lava

Cooled magma
(solid rock)

◀ Some solids need a great amount of heat to change them into a liquid. Deep inside the earth, very high temperatures melt solid rock. The liquid rock is called magma. When a volcano erupts, the magma – now lava – shoots out and flows down the side of the volcano. When it cools to about 1,500°F, it becomes solid rock again.

EVAPORATING AND CONDENSING

cooling
condensing
Heating
Evaporating

Gas

When a liquid is heated, the pull between molecules may be completely broken, making the molecules free to float away. Molecules from the surface of the liquid change into gas and escape into the air. This is called evaporation.

When a gas is cooled, the forces between molecules become stronger and the material changes to a liquid. This is called condensation.

Water evaporates from the ▶ clothes on a clothesline. This is why the clothes dry. Water molecules from rivers, seas, plants, and animals rise into the air as an invisible gas. As the air cools, the gas molecules are drawn together again and condense into tiny drops of water. These form huge clouds in the sky. The clouds may drop their liquid to earth as rain.

WOW!
Even metals evaporate. Tungsten turns into a gas at an astoundingly hot 10,706°F.

11

CHEMICAL CHANGES

You might think of chemicals as just nasty-smelling gases or colored, bubbling liquids. But everything is made of chemicals – even you and this book. Chemicals are simply collections of molecules.

Molecules from different substances will often join together. This is called a chemical change or reaction, and it produces completely new materials.

When leaves turn brown in autumn,

when you bake a cake,

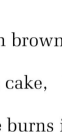

or when gasoline burns in a motorcycle engine,

a chemical change is taking place.

When you slice an apple, it's a good idea to eat it quickly. Once it is cut, the inside of the apple turns brown because of a chemical change. Oxygen in the air reacts with the newly cut surface of the apple to produce a brown chemical.

Chemical changes happen at different speeds. Some are very slow, like the one that occurs when dough rises. Others are very fast. The brilliant bursts from fireworks happen as part of explosive chemical reactions.

RUSTING

◀ When iron or steel objects, like these cogs, are left in a wet place, they combine slowly with oxygen and water. The chemical reaction produces a new, reddish compound of iron and oxygen called rust, or iron oxide. Other chemicals, like the salt in the air at the beach, may speed up the rusting reaction.

The chemical change that happens when rust is formed can be shown like this:

Iron + Oxygen + Water = Iron oxide   Water

Paint on cars and bicycles protects their iron frames from water and oxygen, which cause rust. Sometimes iron is galvanized instead of painted – it is coated with zinc, which doesn't react with oxygen and water to form rust.

Imagine how nasty it would be to eat with a rusty knife and fork. Cutlery is often made of stainless steel. This is steel that has had some chromium mixed into it. The chromium stops the rusting reaction.

Investigate rusting

1 Collect four jars. Put a nail in each jar.
2 Leave one nail dry. Cover another one completely with water. Drip a little water into the third jar, but don't cover the nail completely. Drip some salt water

Jar with nail

1

A little water

3

Water

2

A little salt water or vinegar

4

or vinegar into the fourth jar.

Which nail gets rusty most quickly?

BURNING

To make a fire three things must be present: heat, oxygen, and something to burn. As soon as one of these is taken away, the fire will go out.

Materials like wood, oil, and plastic are made mainly from carbon. When carbon burns with lots of oxygen from the air, there is a chemical reaction. The gas carbon dioxide is one of the materials that is made.

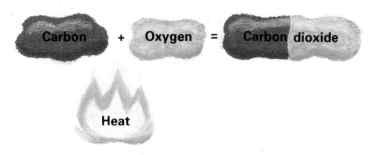

Carbon + Oxygen = Carbon dioxide

Heat

Usually there is not enough oxygen to combine with all the carbon. The extra carbon and other chemicals turn into thick black clouds of smoke and soot.

When gasoline is burned in a car engine, many gases are produced. Some of these, such as nitrous oxides, are poisonous and cause air pollution. ▼

▲ Firefighters pump lots of water onto a burning building. The water takes away the heat of the fire. If not for the firefighters, the fire would live until there was nothing left to burn.

What happens when a candle burns?

Before you blow out the candles on your birthday cake, look carefully at the candle flame. You will see three different areas: bright yellow at the top, blue around the bottom, and clear around the wick.

Candle wax is the candle's fuel. The candle wax must be changed from a solid to a liquid and, finally, to a gas before it will burn. The invisible part of the flame is the gas that has evaporated from the melted wax. The blue part of the flame is burning very fast because air from beneath is rushing up to take the place of the air that is being used up by the flame. The yellow area is where the carbon burns most brightly.

◀ Candles and lamps are often used in religious celebrations. During the Hindu Festival of Light, called Diwali, people fill small clay lamps with oil and light them. They arrange the lamps along the tops of their temples and houses. Some of the lamps are floated on streams and rivers.

D I S S O L V I N G

This sugar cube is dissolving in water. ▶
Sugar is made up of small, regular shapes, called crystals. When water molecules come near the crystals, they break apart each crystal shape. The sugar dissolves in the water and disappears. No chemical reaction has taken place; there is simply a solution of sugar (which is called the solute) and water (the solvent).

Dissolving in hot and cold

Heat helps solids to dissolve quickly because the solvent's molecules have more energy to break the solute apart.

Warm water

Cold water

Sugar

1 Fill two jars, one with warm water and one with cold water.
2 Add a teaspoon of sugar to each and stir both at the same time. Which teaspoon of sugar dissolves first?

◀ Gases can be dissolved in liquids and can even be frozen in them. Look closely at some ice cubes and you will see bubbles in them. This scientist is about to test a piece of ice from the Antarctic for dissolved gases. The gases he finds will give him information about climate changes in the past and increases in air pollution.

◀ Rainwater can dissolve limestone rock. When the water that has dissolved the limestone drips into a cave, the limestone comes out of solution and gradually forms beautiful shapes called stalactites and stalagmites. The stalactites in the Carlsbad Caverns in New Mexico have taken more than 10 million years to grow this big.

Epsom salts

2 cups warm water

Make your own stalactites

1 Dissolve as much Epsom salts as you can in about 2 cups of warm water.
2 Fill two glasses with the solution.
3 Hang a cotton string between the two glasses. Make sure each end of the string is in the solution. Put a small saucer underneath the string.
4 Over a few days, watch the stalactites form as the water drips off the string.

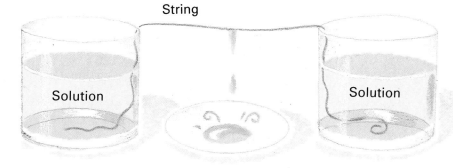

String

Solution

Solution

Saucer

ALL MIXED UP

Substances can be mixed together. If no chemical reaction takes place, no new substances are formed. Instead, a mixture has been made.

Salt and sand

1 Mix together a large spoonful of salt and a spoonful of sand. Stir them well. Now see if you can separate the salt from the sand in the mixture. You could do it – but it would take ages.

There is a quick way to separate the sand and salt.

2 Pour the mixture into a large jar. Add plenty of warm water. Screw on the lid and shake the jar. What happens?

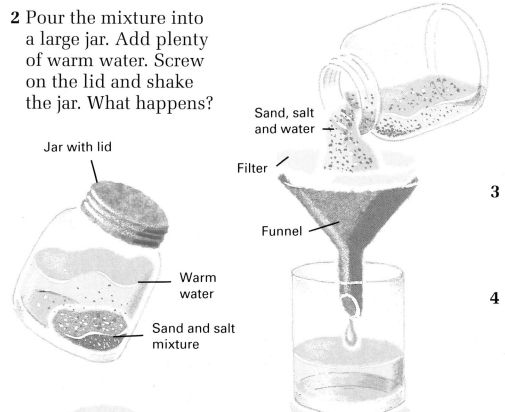

Shallow bowl

Jar with lid

Sand, salt and water

Filter

Funnel

Warm water

Sand and salt mixture

3 Slowly pour the contents of the jar through a small coffee filter. Notice the sand stays on the filter.

4 Pour the solution that came through the filter into a shallow bowl. Let it evaporate. What substance is left?

When the liquid (solvent) in a solution evaporates away, the solid (solute) is left behind. These shallow, salty ponds in Brazil are called salt pans. They are dried in the sun, and, as the water evaporates, the salt comes out of the solution. The salt is collected and used.

Gold is a metal that does not react easily with other materials. This is why it keeps its precious shine and can be found as pure gold nuggets.

◀ These old-time miners in Australia are panning for gold. Sieves and water were used to wash away the lighter rock and earth, leaving the small but heavier gold pieces behind.

ACIDS AND ALKALIS

Have you ever eaten rhubarb? If you have, you may have noticed that it made your teeth feel funny. This is because rhubarb contains a lot of acid – much more than most fruits. Acids are usually sour tasting and will react with other materials by eating away at them. The acid in rhubarb reacts with the other chemicals in your mouth.

Make your own chemical indicator

1 Tear up some red cabbage leaves into a bowl.
2 Ask an adult to help you add some hot water and use a spoon to squeeze the color from the leaves.

Some acids, such as vinegar and lemon juice, are weak. Others, like the acid in a car battery, are strong and highly dangerous. If a very powerful acid splashes on you, it can eat away your skin like a burn.

The chemical opposite of an acid is an alkali. Alkalis make good cleaning materials. Laundry soap and dishwashing liquid are alkaline. People often clean drains with caustic soda because it is a very strong alkali and can eat away dirt.

It is useful to have a safe way of telling whether something is acidic or alkaline. One way to tell is to use a dye called a chemical indicator. The dye changes color depending on whether it is mixed with an acid or an alkali.

Red cabbage

Hot water

3 Let the purple water cool.
4 Pour a little of your indicator into a jar. Add a spoonful of fruit juice and watch the color change. Acids turn the indicator red and alkalis will make it purple again.

Fruit juice

Cabbage water

When you mix an acid and an alkali they cancel each other out. Sometimes your stomach makes too much acid and you feel sick. To make yourself feel better you can take a weak alkali, such as sodium bicarbonate. As the acid and alkali react they produce carbon dioxide, which can make you burp.

▲ This farmer is spreading lime, which is alkaline, on soil that is too acidic. When rain falls, the lime will dissolve and make the soil less acidic. This will help to produce better crops next season.

Make a volcano

In this activity you can see exciting results when a weak acid reacts with a weak alkali.

1 On an old tray, make a volcano with a hollow on top from modeling clay or play dough.
2 Put a small amount of sodium bicarbonate into the hollow. Add a few drops of red food coloring.

3 Slowly drip in some vinegar. Watch your volcano erupt as the acidic vinegar reacts with the alkaline sodium bicarbonate.

Red food coloring and sodium bicarbonate

Volcano made from modeling clay or play dough

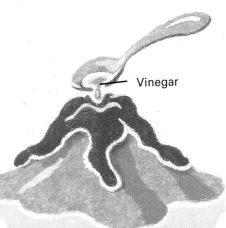

Vinegar

ELASTIC
AND PLASTIC
MATERIALS

Try stretching a rubber band and watch it spring back to its original shape. Rubber is an elastic material. However much you stretch or squeeze the rubber, forces between the molecules always want to pull it back into place.

A lot of balls are made from rubbery material. Most bounce really well because as soon as the ball is squashed or hit the elastic material tries to spring back into shape. ▼

▲ Bows are made of elastic materials. The archer pulls the bow out of shape. The force of the bow as it springs back into shape sends the arrow flying through the air.

You would probably be surprised at some of the substances that have elastic properties. Materials like steel, concrete, glass, and wood are elastic, even though they are hard. If they were completely rigid, most buildings and bridges would collapse when blown by high winds or shaken by earthquakes.

San Francisco is built ▶ in an area that occasionally suffers terrible earthquakes. The designers of new buildings in San Francisco, such as of the Transamerica Pyramid, are careful to choose elastic materials and flexible structures that will stand up to the forces of an earthquake.

Some materials can be pinched, squeezed, and pulled into new shapes. These materials are said to be plastic. They take on the new shape and don't change back. The molecules are fixed in a rigid structure. Wet clay is a good example of a very plastic material. ◀

People shape all kinds of materials into new and useful objects. We even call a whole group of materials "plastic" because we are able to mold and shape them.

THE MOLECULES OF LIFE

You are surrounded by a variety of living things. Think how different they all are; the green leaf of a tree is nothing like the soft fur of a cat. Yet, while living things may look very different, they are in fact all made up of the same basic elements – carbon, oxygen, hydrogen, and nitrogen. It is the way these elements behave that gives useful properties to so many materials.

Plants give us many raw materials. Some trees are chopped down for their wood to make things like furniture and paper. Others produce useful things that can be harvested. Latex is collected from under the bark of certain tropical trees to make rubber, and all around the world trees provide fruit.

▲ Cork is taken from the bark of living oak trees that grow in the warm countries of southern Europe and Australia. The bark is so thick that sheets of it can be stripped off without harming the tree.

◄ The cotton plant, with its fluffy, white seed heads, grows in very hot places like Egypt, India, and the southern United States. When the seed heads have been picked and cleaned, the long cotton fibers are spun into threads that can be woven into cloth.

WOW!
During World War II (1939–45), Russia was not able to get rubber from abroad. Instead, the Russians used the milky sap from dandelions to make rubber.

People began hunting animals in prehistoric times. They used every part of the animals: the meat for food, fat for fuel, skins for clothes, and bones for tools.

From the seventeenth century ▶ onwards, whales were hunted in larger and larger numbers. They provided hundreds of useful products. Their oil was used to make soaps, perfumes, and candles. Their bones were used in corsets and the hoops in ladies' dresses. Today, many species of whale are in danger of becoming extinct because too many have been killed.

Animals provide us with many fibers to make cloth. The silkworm spins itself a safe cocoon in which it can change into a moth, and so complete part of its life cycle. We get silk by unwinding the cocoon before the moth escapes. Up to two miles of thread comes from one cocoon. The Chinese discovered how to make silk thousands of years ago. They guarded the secret, and anyone who carried silkworms or their eggs out of China was punished by death. ▼

WOW!

A spider's silk is twice as strong as a strand of aluminum of the same thickness. It is also a lot more elastic.

MATERIALS FROM THE EARTH

The earth's outer layer, or crust, holds ▶ clues about how the land has been formed and changed over millions and millions of years. Everything, from the highest mountains to the widest valleys, is made up of many different types of minerals and rocks.

▲ The pyramids on the Giza Plateau in Egypt have been standing for nearly 4,500 years. The ancient Egyptian kings, or pharaohs, had them built from enormous stone blocks cut from the ground. The pyramids were built as royal burial tombs while the pharaohs were still alive. They were filled with numerous treasures – even things to eat and drink – for the pharaohs to take with them to the afterworld when they died.

Most metals come from minerals called ores that are dug from the ground. Usually the shiny metal looks nothing like the dull ore from which it is taken.

◀ In early times, getting metals from ores must have seemed like magic. Many myths grew up around metalworking. In Viking mythology, Thor was the strongest god. He was imagined as a huge blacksmith who shaped metal into weapons. Viking people thought that thunder was the sound of Thor's hammering. The Roman god of fire and metal-making was Vulcan. A fire-spurting volcano was believed to be his workshop.

Glass is made by melting together sand, lime, and soda. All these materials are dug out of the ground. The molten (liquid) glass can be made into very intricate shapes before it cools.

Glass can be a strong, flexible material ▶ when it is turned into very thin strands called fibers. We use glass fiber in many different ways. Notice the points of light at the ends of these glass fibers. These are called fiber-optic strands, and each one is as thin as a hair. Fiber-optic strands can be used to carry light beams for many miles. They can also be used to see inside people's bodies without having to cut them open.

Many fuels come from the earth. Coal, oil, and natural gas (methane) are formed beneath the earth's surface from dead plant and animal material. They take millions of years to form, and today we are using them quicker than they are being made.

◀ At this natural gas processing plant, methane is being refined and stored ready for us to use. Methane can be burned as a fuel or turned into useful products.

SYNTHETIC MATERIALS

Some scientists mix raw materials to make completely new substances that don't exist in the natural world. These are synthetic materials. They can have many useful properties.

Most plastics are made from oil and gas found beneath the earth's surface, but some are made from wood, cotton, milk, or other natural materials. Plastics have thousands of uses, such as for these items shown here.

Nylon is a kind of plastic. It was the first synthetic fiber ever made. The way to make nylon was discovered in 1938 as a result of experiments to find out how molecules are formed in nature.

Can you follow the nylon-making process?

Nylon, like other plastics, is made from the elements carbon, hydrogen, oxygen, and nitrogen, which make up all living things. Oil, natural gas, water, and even oats and corn cobs can be made into nylon. The properties of different elements allow them to link up and combine to make giant chains of molecules. These chains make a very tough material that can be heated and stretched to make nylon fibers.

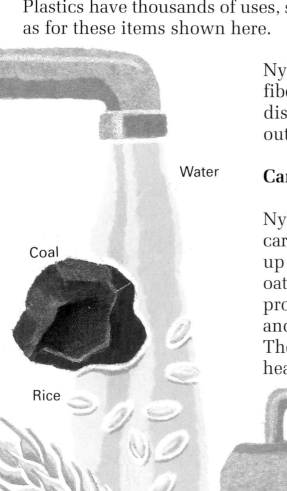

Water

Coal

Rice

Oats

The chemicals needed to make nylon are mixed together.

Materials containing carbon fibers are now used to make sports equipment. The material for skis needs to be light, strong, and flexible.

Although fibers are thin, they can be very strong when put together. To see this for yourself, tug a single nylon thread until it snaps. Then see how difficult it is to snap a few threads that have been put together.

The threads are stretched on rollers.

The mixture is melted and the liquid is pushed through tiny holes, like water in a shower.

The thin nylon fibers are wound onto bobbins ready to make cloth.

Cold air is blown over the jets of warm liquid. They become hard nylon threads.

GLOSSARY

Atom   The very smallest particle of a substance that can exist by itself.

Bonds   Invisible forces that hold atoms or molecules together.

Burning   The chemical reaction between materials and air that produces a lot of heat.

Compound   A substance that is made up of two or more elements.

Condensation   The process in which a gas cools to become a liquid.

Crystals   Small, regular shapes that are created by the structure of molecules in a material.

Elements   Substances made up of only one type of atom. There are more than 110 known elements in existence.

Evaporation   The process in which a liquid changes to a gas.

Extinct   Something that used to live on the earth but has died out.

Flexible   Something that can bend without breaking.

Force   A push or a pull. There are forces (or bonds) between atoms and molecules that hold them together.

Gas   A material in which the molecules are spaced wide apart and move freely.

Life cycle   The series of changes a plant or animal goes through during its life.

Liquid   A material in which the molecules move about, making it runny. A liquid takes the shape of the container it is in.

Melt   To change from a solid to a liquid by heating.

Minerals   These are substances that exist in nature and are found in things like rock.

Molecule   Two or more atoms bonded together.

Particle   A tiny part of a substance.

Properties   The ways a substance looks, feels, and behaves.

Raw materials   Materials found in nature that can be used for making other things.

Refining   Processing and cleaning a substance.

Solid   A material in which all the molecules have a fixed position.

Solute   A material that will dissolve.

Solution   A liquid in which the solute has become dissolved by the solvent.

Solvent   A liquid that will cause another substance to dissolve.

Stalactites   Long columns of limestone hanging from a cave roof.

Stalagmites   Columns of limestone building up from a cave floor.

Synthetic   Made by people; not naturally occurring.

BOOKS TO READ

Barber, Jacqueline. *Solids, Liquids, and Gases*. Berkeley: Lawrence Science, 1986.

Berger, Melvin. *Our Atomic World*. First Books. New York: Franklin Watts, 1988.

Dyson, Susan. *Wood*. Resources. New York: Thomson Learning, 1993.

Friedhoffer, Robert. *Matter and Energy*. Scientific Magic. New York: Franklin Watts, 1992.

Friedhoffer, Robert. *Molecules and Heat*. Scientific Magic. New York: Franklin Watts, 1992.

Jackman, Wayne. *Gas*. Resources. New York: Thomson Learning, 1993.

Jackman, Wayne. *Plastics*. Resources. New York: Thomson Learning, 1993.

Jennings, Terry. *Heat*. The Young Scientist Investigates. Chicago: Childrens Press, 1989.

Jennings, Terry. *Materials*. The Young Scientist Investigates. Chicago: Childrens Press, 1989.

Lefferty, Peter. *Burning and Melting: Projects With Heat*. Hands On Science. New York: Gloucester Press, 1990.

Langley, Andrew. *Steel*. Resources. New York: Thomson Learning, 1993.

Parker, Steve. *Chemistry*. Fun With Science. New York: Warwick Press, 1990.

Rickard, Graham. *Bricks* . Resources. New York: Thomson Learning, 1993.

Rickard, Graham. *Oil*. Resources. New York: Thomson Learning, 1993.

Songhurst, Hazel. *Glass*. Resources. New York: Thomson Learning, 1993.

Taylor, Barbara. *Structures and Materials*. Science Starters. New York: Franklin Watts, 1991.

INDEX